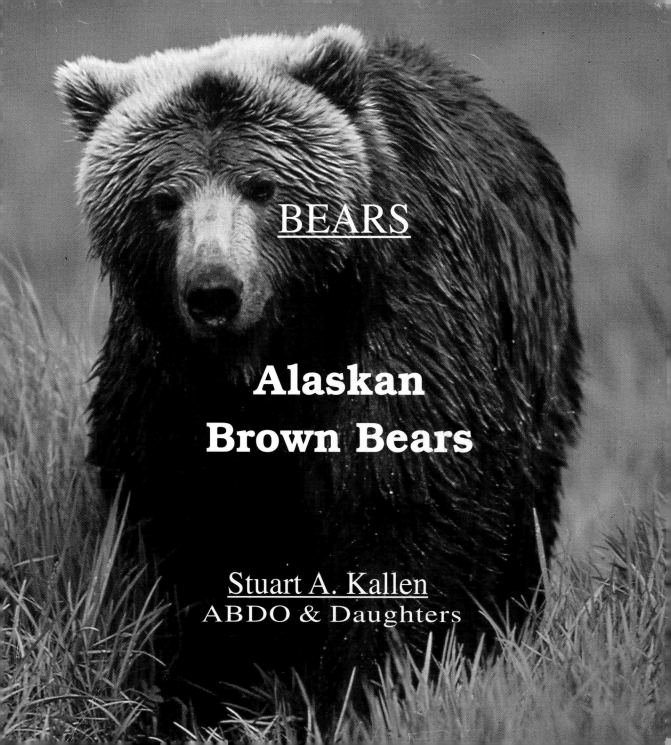

BEARS

Alaskan Brown Bears

Stuart A. Kallen
ABDO & Daughters

visit us at
www.abdopub.com

Published by Abdo & Daughters, 4940 Viking Drive, Suite 622, Edina, Minnesota 55435.

Copyright © 1998 by Abdo Consulting Group, Inc., Pentagon Tower, P.O. Box 36036, Minneapolis, Minnesota 55435 USA. International copyrights reserved in all countries. No part of this book may be reproduced in any form without written permission from the publisher.

Printed in the United States.

Cover Photo credits: Peter Arnold, Inc.
Interior Photo credits: Peter Arnold, Inc.

Edited by Lori Kinstad Pupeza

Library of Congress Cataloging-in-Publication Data

Kallen, Stuart A., 1955-
    Alaskan brown bears / Stuart A. Kallen.
    P.   cm. -- (Bears)
    Includes index.
    Summary: Briefly describes the physical characteristics, the habitat, and the behavior of the Alaskan brown bear.
    ISBN 1-56239-595-5
    1. Kodiak bear--Juvenile literature. 2. Brown bear--Alaskan--Juvenile literature.
    [1. Kodiak bear. 2. Brown bear. 3. Bears.] I. Title. II. Series: Kallen, Stuart A., 1955-   Bears..
    QL737.C27K335   1998
    599.74'446--dc20   96-3802
                                                                      CIP
                                                                      AC

Contents

Alaskan Brown Bears and Family

Bears are **mammals**. Like humans, they breathe air with lungs, are **warm blooded**, and **nurse** their young with milk.

Bears first appeared 40 million years ago. They were small, meat-eating, tree-climbing animals. The early bears were related to coyotes, wolves, foxes, raccoons, and dogs.

Today, there are eight different kinds of bear. They live in 50 countries in 3 **continents**. Alaskan brown bears are not the greatest hunters. Eighty-five percent of their diet is made up of vegetables. The Alaskan brown bear is a member of the brown bear family.

Opposite page: Three Alaskan brown bears.

Size, Shape, and Color

Alaskan brown bears are the largest bears in North America. The average adult is 7 to 10 feet tall (2.1 to 3.1 m) when standing on its hind legs. Brown bears may weigh from 500 to 900 pounds (226 to 408 kg). Males are about 50 percent larger than females.

Alaskan brown bears are stout with a large hump of fat and muscle over the shoulders. They have large heads, wide faces, small eyes, and powerful jaws.

Alaskan brown bears are usually dark brown to almost black. Sometimes the tips of the hair are white. The fur is long and thick.

Alaskan brown bears have long, curved claws and large, pointed teeth that help them catch and kill **prey**.

Opposite page: An Alaskan brown bear standing.

Where They Live

Alaskan brown bears are found in Alaska. They live on the coastal areas and Kodiak Island. No one knows exactly how many Alaskan brown bears there are, but the guess is about 30,000 to 40,000.

Alaskan brown bears preying on salmon.

Senses

Bears are smart animals that learn quickly. They are curious and have good memories.

Though they have small eyes, brown bears have good eyesight. They can tell the difference between colors and see well at night. They can spot moving objects at a far distance. Bears stand on their hind legs to see farther. They also hear well.

The Alaskan brown bears' keen sense of smell allows them to find mates, avoid humans, find their **cubs**, and gather food. Bears have been known to detect a human scent 14 hours after a person has passed along a trail. And they can smell food three miles (4.8 km) away!

Opposite page: A female Alaskan brown bear resting.

Defense

Alaskan brown bears are powerful creatures. They move rocks and large logs with one paw. No animal of an equal size is as strong. A brown bear may kill a moose, elk, or deer with a single blow to the neck. It may then carry the animal in its mouth for many miles.

Alaskan brown bears are surprisingly quick. They can easily run 35 to 40 mph (56 to 64 kmph) for short distances.

Most bears would rather run away from a human than attack. Bears attack when protecting their young, if their escape route is blocked, if they are protecting food sources, or if they are startled.

Opposite page: Alaskan brown bears fighting.

Food

Alaskan brown bears eat just about anything. To fuel such huge bodies, they must eat 80 or 90 pounds (36 to 41 kg) of food every day during the summer.

Alaskan brown bears are well-known for their salmon fishing. They plunge into racing rivers and grab salmon swimming upstream to **spawn**. A fishing bear may eat up to 12 or more large salmon in one afternoon.

Alaskan brown bears will also eat food that has been left on the sand by the ocean. This may be seaweed, mollusks, crabs, and washed up bodies of animals like seals. Away from the water, brown bears will eat moose, deer, elk, caribou, and plants.

An Alaskan brown bear eating salmon.

Hibernation

As summer ends, Alaskan brown bears may have 6 to 10 inches (15 to 25 cm) of fat under their skin. They also drink huge amounts of water.

As winter comes, Alaskan brown bears find **dens** in caves or hollow areas under large trees. The den must be far away from humans. Noise from snowmobiles and airplanes will drive a bear further into the wilderness.

By the middle of October, Alaskan brown bears are fast asleep—**hibernating** in their dens. When spring comes, they wake up.

The bears weigh about half as much as they did in the fall. They are hungry and need to drink plenty of water. Soon they are looking for berries, roots, herbs, and new grasses.

A sleepy Alaskan brown bear and her cub.

Babies

Bears usually mate in June and July. Female bears are **pregnant** for about eight months. **Cubs** are born in the winter while the mother is sleeping in the **den**.

Usually two cubs are born. They weigh 8.5 to 11.5 ounces (240 to 330 g). The cubs are blind, bald, and helpless.

When they are five weeks old, cubs can walk. By springtime, they are ready to leave the den. This is a dangerous time. The cubs may be killed by eagles, bobcats, and mountain lions.

When they are 6 months old, bear cubs weigh 55 to 65 pounds (25 to 30 kg). The cubs will spend two winters in the den with their mother. After that, the mother will force them out.

Alaskan brown bear cubs.

Alaskan Brown Bear Facts

Scientific Name: *Ursus arctos.*

Average Size: The average adult is 35 to 60 inches tall (89 to 127 cm) when standing on all 4 feet. Brown bears are about 7 to 10 feet (2.1 to 3.1 m) when standing up on their hind legs.

They may weigh from 500 to 900 pounds (226 to 408 kg). Males are about 50 percent larger than females. The largest Alaskan brown bear ever recorded weighed 2,500 pounds (1,132 kg).

Where They're Found: There are about 30,000 to 40,000 Alaskan brown bears living in the coastal areas of Alaska and near the **Arctic Circle**.

Glossary

Arctic Circle - the very cold region near the North Pole.

continent (KAHN-tih-nent) - one of the seven main land masses: Europe, Asia, Africa, North America, South America, Australia, and Antarctica.

cub - a baby bear.

den - a cave, hole in the ground, or hole in a tree used by a bear for a shelter.

hibernate (HI-bur-nate) - to spend the winter in a deep sleep.

mammal (MAM-ull) - a class of animals, including humans, that have hair and feed their young milk.

nurse - to feed a young animal or child milk from the mother's breast.

pregnant - with one or more babies growing inside the mother's body.

prey (PRAY) - an animal hunted and captured for food.

spawn - the cycle when fish lay eggs to reproduce.

warm blooded - an animal whose body temperature remains the same and warmer than the outside air or temperature.

Index